BEYOND GERONIMO THE APACHE EXPERIENCE

EXHIBITION CATALOGUE

Janet Cantley

Published by the Heard Museum
Phoenix, Arizona

ISBN 978-0-934351-86-7 (hardcover)

Printed in Phoenix, AZ by Ironwood Lithographers, Inc.

Beyond Geronimo: The Apache Experience is
published through the generous support of
William and Jo Elizabeth Ridenour.

STAFF ACKNOWLEDGEMENTS FOR PUBLICATION:
Janet Cantley, Curator
Caesar Chaves, Creative Director
Yukiko Corella, IIDA, Exhibit Designer
Phil Douglass, Exhibit Construction Specialist
Kelsey Hage, Graphic Designer
Ann Marshall, Ph.D., Vice President Curation and Education
Marcus Monenerkit, Associate Registrar
Craig Smith, Photographer
Jim Weaver, Director Major Gifts

This publication was produced in conjunction with
the exhibit, *Beyond Geronimo: The Apache Experience*,
an official Arizona Centennial Legacy project sponsored
by J.P. Morgan, Chase, Boeing, Republic Services,
APS, Ridenour, Hienton & Lewis, LLC.; Richard and
Mary Anne Cree, The Ann B. Ritt Estate, and
anonymous benefactors.

EXHIBIT DATES AT THE HEARD MUSEUM:
February 11, 2012 to January 20, 2013

Dimensions of artwork are given in inches.
For two-dimensional works of art, width precedes
height; depth follows for three-dimensional pieces.

COVER:
Edward S. Curtis, photographer
"Geronimo, taken the day before he rode in President
Theodore Roosevelt's Inaugural Parade," 1905.
Heard Museum RC 28(1):2

IMAGES FOR PUBLICATION COURTESY OF:
Billie Jane Baguley Library and Archives, Heard Museum
Allan Houser Inc
Arizona Historical Society/Tucson
Department of Anthropology, Smithsonian Institution
National Museum of the American Indian Archives
Oklahoma Historical Society Archives
Phoenix Public Library, Arizona Room

OBJECT LOANS ILLUSTRATED IN PUBLICATION COURTESY OF:
Amerind Foundation
Autry National Center
Arizona State Museum
Chiinde
Penny Cleghorn-Soontay
Dustinn Craig
Oliver Enjady
Bob Haozous
Phillip M. Haozous/Saayo Povi Fine Art
Vincent Kaydahzinne and Family
Douglas Miles
Native American Connections
National Museum of the American Indian,
    Smithsonian Institution
National Museum of Natural History,
    Smithsonian Institution
Nohwike'Bagowa Museum,
    White Mountain Apache Tribe
William and Jo Elizabeth Ridenour
Rennard Strickland
Jane and Ed Ulery

CONTENTS

FOREWORD

The Apache story, like the history of so many tribes, reflects the internal difficulties that tribes encountered as they tried to coexist in their own homelands with the settlers and other newcomers who came to live in "Indian country." The deep fissures in tribal governance that occurred as tribes tried to deal with these intrusions by peaceful means at times, and as warrior defenders of their homes at others, created division and discord within tribes and among tribes, some of which has carried over into more recent times.

Beyond Geronimo: The Apache Experience deals with this issue in a very straightforward manner. This exhibit was ably curated by Janet Cantley, and it shows great insight into the dilemma of the people and the aftermath of the Apache Wars, as well as the sad plight of those who were prisoners of war for decades. The exhibit is rich with artifacts of the time of Geronimo, and special praise goes to Marcus Monenerkit, the registrar for this exhibit, who arranged for borrowing so many pieces and their proper handling. The exhibit also uses contemporary art by Apache artists to express—through painting, sculpture and other media—the cultural impact of this period.

The Heard design team, led by Creative Director Caesar Chaves, has again created an appealing and compelling exhibit, and Yukiko Corella, who was the lead designer for this exhibit, has created a new standard of excellence. Kelsey Hage has made this beautiful catalogue and she along with Sarah Moore artfully created graphics for the exhibit. The design team creates all casework and other presentation materials for Heard exhibits in-house; Phil Douglass and Dan Johnson are the fabricators who do such superb work. We are fortunate to have the accomplished photographer, Craig Smith, at the Heard. He took most of the object photographs, scanned many of the historic images and made the in-gallery panoramas.

Finally, many thanks are due to the many individuals and institutions who loaned materials for this exhibit, particularly to William and Jo Elizabeth Ridenour who not only loaned many special artifacts, but also funded this book, and to the exhibit sponsors, listed in the frontpiece. The Heard is deeply grateful for the support of these individuals and organizations.

Letitia Chambers

Dr. Letitia Chambers
President & CEO of the Heard Museum

INTRODUCTION

As an Arizona Centennial Legacy Project *Beyond Geronimo: the Apache Experience* focuses on 19th and 20th century Chiricahua and Western Apache history and events leading up to statehood. In addition, to illustrate the thriving artistic traditions that continue today, we present 20th and 21st century Apache artists reflecting on the historical events and cultural traditions that shape Apache identity today.

In planning an exhibit that went "beyond Geronimo," we consulted with individuals from Apache communities at Fort Sill, Oklahoma, Mescalero, New Mexico, and the White Mountain, Dilzhe'e and San Carlos Tribes in Arizona. Artists from those communities loaned work for the exhibit. We also consulted authors and museum professionals from as far as England and, of course, some more local. Private individuals donated art specifically for this exhibit. Object loans came from twelve institutions and twelve individuals. We requested images from seven library archives. We are grateful to the many institutions and individuals and their generosity which made this exhibit possible.

I am grateful to a number of people who have given support, directly and indirectly, and in innumerable ways, to this project. I appreciate the dedicated team of people I work with on a daily basis at the Heard Museum. No exhibit opens without the assistance of every staff member. Together we can do much.

Janet Cantley

Janet Cantley
Curator at the Heard Museum

SECTION 1

INTRODUCTION

The name "Geronimo" is known internationally as the legendary Apache warrior, and also as a synonym for anything "Apache." But few people know the mixed emotions and many perspectives on Geronimo held by Apache people—who he was, how he lived, why he did what he did, and how that affected the Chiricahua Apache and other Apache tribes. For some Apache, Geronimo possessed qualities that are strongly admired—a protector of tribal lands who demonstrated courage, strength and determination, and skill as a warrior and shaman.

He was never a hero among many Apache. Others blame him for the removal and punishment of all Chiricahua Apache, who received a 28-year sentence as prisoners of war and permanent exile from Arizona. He was unyielding in seeking revenge for real and perceived wrongs to his family.

In the exhibit and accompanying catalogue we seek to shine a light on other Apache leaders, many who remain largely unknown today, to reveal their art, personal items and images, and to dispel some of the myths surrounding the larger-than-life figure of Geronimo.

Contemporary artists through a variety of media reflect on Apache experiences leading up to Arizona Statehood and are inspired by continuing cultural traditions to tell stories of courage and endurance.

Yukiko Corella, exhibit designer; Craig Smith, photographer
The entrance to *Beyond Geronimo: the Apache Experience*, Heard Museum.

Allan Houser
Chiricahua (Warm Springs)
Apache, 1914–1994
The Future, 1985
Bronze; edition of 6; 31 x 45 x 24

Allan Houser is a renowned
painter and sculptor, one of the
first born after the Chiricahua
release as prisoners of war.
A strong theme in Houser's art
is the family-centered nature of
Apache people.

Collection of Chiinde

WHO ARE THE APACHE?

The term "Apache" is applied to any of six separate but related tribes, each with its own territory and its own history. These tribes are:

- Western Apache
- Chiricahua Apache
- Mescalero Apache
- Jicarilla Apache
- Lipan Apache
- Kiowa-Apache

The Apache tribes' territories existed in parts of areas that are now called Arizona, New Mexico, Texas, Colorado, Kansas, Oklahoma and northern states of Mexico, Sonora and Chihuahua.

Because of different interactions with the United States government and military, the histories of the six tribes further diverge.

- The U.S. government divided the Western Apache tribe into four politically separate entities (San Carlos Apache, White Mountain Apache, Payson Tonto Apache and Camp Verde Yavapai-Apache), each with its own reservation.

- The Chiricahua Apache tribe was divided into two parts, with one forming the Fort Sill Apache Tribe and the other part joining with the Mescalero Apache and the remnants of the Lipan Apache to form the modern Mescalero Apache Tribe. The Fort Sill Apache have tribal headquarters near Apache, Oklahoma, and the federal government has recently returned 30 acres of tribal land near Deming, New Mexico.

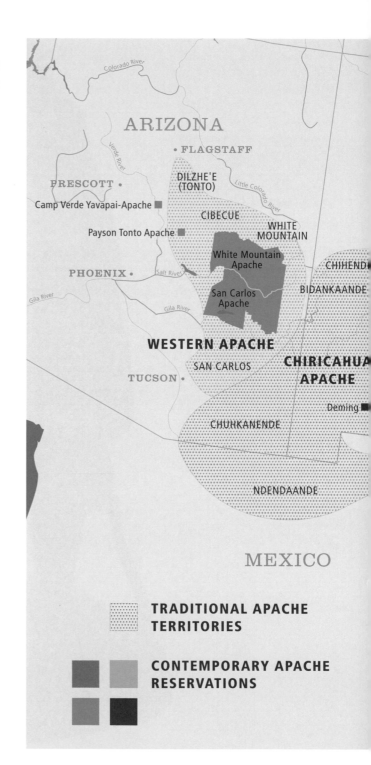

ARIZONA

- FLAGSTAFF

PRESCOTT •

DILZHE'E (TONTO)

Camp Verde Yavapai-Apache ■

CIBECUE

WHITE MOUNTAIN

Payson Tonto Apache ■

White Mountain Apache

CHIHEND

BIDANKAANDE

PHOENIX •   Salt River

San Carlos Apache

Gila River

Gila River

WESTERN APACHE

SAN CARLOS

CHIRICAHUA APACHE

TUCSON •

Deming ■

CHUHKANENDE

NDENDAANDE

MEXICO

▦ **TRADITIONAL APACHE TERRITORIES**

■ **CONTEMPORARY APACHE RESERVATIONS**

MAP OF TRADITIONAL AND CONTEMPORARY APACHE LANDS

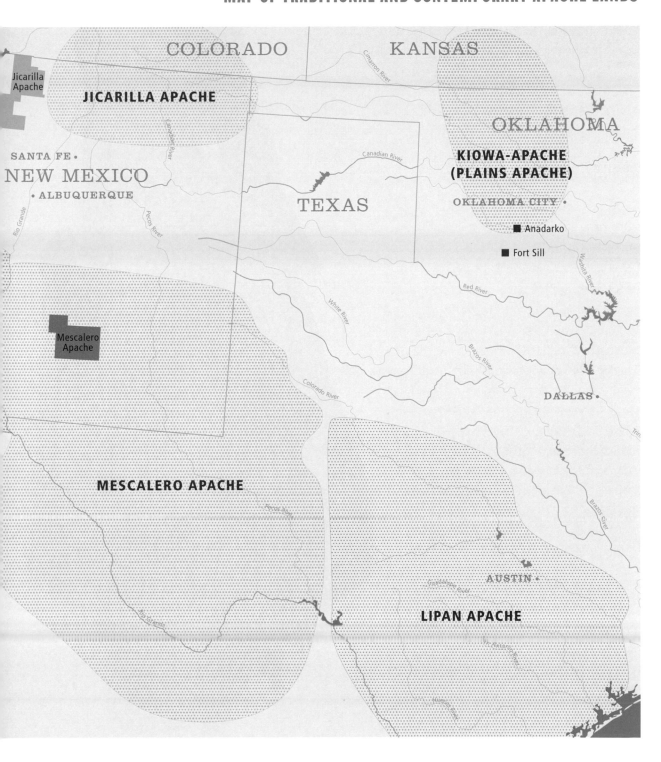

COLORADO

KANSAS

Jicarilla Apache

JICARILLA APACHE

OKLAHOMA

SANTA FE •
NEW MEXICO

KIOWA-APACHE (PLAINS APACHE)

• ALBUQUERQUE

OKLAHOMA CITY •

TEXAS

■ Anadarko

■ Fort Sill

Rio Grande

Pecos River

Canadian River

Cimarron River

Washita River

Red River

White River

Brazos River

Mescalero Apache

MESCALERO APACHE

DALLAS •

Colorado River

AUSTIN •

LIPAN APACHE

- The Jicarilla Apache Tribe has its own reservation in northern New Mexico.

- The Kiowa-Apache are now known as the Apache Tribe of Oklahoma with a tribal headquarters at Anadarko, Oklahoma.

APACHE WOMEN

Women are a mainstay in Apache culture. Kin relationship and residence are based on the female side of the family. Today there are many examples of Apache women in leadership in tribal government and in community activities. White Painted Woman, one of the most important holy beings and the First Woman, gave the Apache the coming-of-age ceremony celebrating a young woman's maturation. This ancient tradition continues today with a four day ceremony that brings together family and friends in support of a young woman's transition to adulthood.

Opposite page: **Mildred Imach Cleghorn**
Fort Sill Apache, 1910–1997
Doll, 1950–1980
Muslin, cotton, embroidery thread, glass beads,
buckskin, feather plume, abalone, rickrack, lace, shell
beads, tin, brass tack, pigment; 6 x 12 x 3

Mildred Imach was born a prisoner of war at Fort Sill,
Oklahoma. She became an educator, dollmaker,
seamstress and then tribal chair of the Fort Sill Apache
from 1976 to 1995. She was a respected leader and
active on the national level in conferences related to
Indian education and preservation of traditional history
and culture. She made dolls as a teaching tool to show
the differences in clothing between the Apache tribes.
The doll shown here is Western Apache or Chiricahua.

Collection of Penny Cleghorn-Soontay

Above: **Chiricahua Apache**
Dolls, c. 1880
Buckskin, horse hair, cotton fabric, tin, glass beads,
brass tacks, pigment; 6 x 12 x 2 and 10 x 17.75 x 2.5

Collection of the Amerind Foundation, 774 & 914

HISTORICAL OVERVIEW

Apache interactions with neighboring Native peoples—including trading, visiting, raiding and warring—changed over time. At various points, Apache traded and made alliances with Spaniards, Mexicans and Americans. But the traditional Apache lifeway requires a great deal of land for survival. Expansion of settlements by both Apache and outsiders created competition for resources, which led to conflicts. For three centuries, Apache people resisted outsiders' occupation, assimilation and annihilation.

After the 1848 war between Mexico and the United States, Americans claimed a large part of Apache territories. American ambition to exploit mineral wealth, build commercial routes to the West Coast and occupy land that had been utilized by Apache led to war.

As part of a "Peace Policy" starting in 1871, the U.S. government confined Apache tribes in Arizona and New Mexico to reservations. There were two basic responses by the Apache to the reservation system: People either accommodated to the regulations and restrictions as a means of survival, or they resisted, by fleeing the reservation and escaping pursuit by the American or Mexican military.

Those who accepted the American presence and stayed on the reservation saw this as a way to keep families together and survive. Some Apache joined the U.S. military as scouts to try to persuade others; they felt that resistance would lead to imprisonment or annihilation.

Others, including Geronimo, refused to submit to the reservations' restrictions and returned to homelands. The Chiricahua Apache had been removed to alien territory when relocated to San Carlos, and the reservation was permeated with fear, distrust and discontent. This led to breakouts, raids and pursuit.

By September 1886, the last Chiricahua resistors, under the leadership of Naiche, learned their relatives had been shipped by train to Florida. They agreed to surrender, with the understanding that they would join their families in Florida for two years and then return to Arizona.

Instead, the Chiricahua Apache were held as prisoners of war for 28 years.

Above: **Yukiko Corella, exhibit designer; Craig Smith, photographer**
Gallery view of Defining Apache section, *Beyond Geronimo: the Apache Experience*, Heard Museum.

Below: **Western Apache**
Awl case, late 19ᵗʰ century
Tanned hide, glass beads, tin, thread, pigment; 4 x 40 x 1.5

Western Apache awl cases typically were ornamented with beads and tin cones. The cases held an awl, an essential tool for repairing moccasins, clothing, a saddlebag or a basket

Collection of William and Jo Elizabeth Ridenour

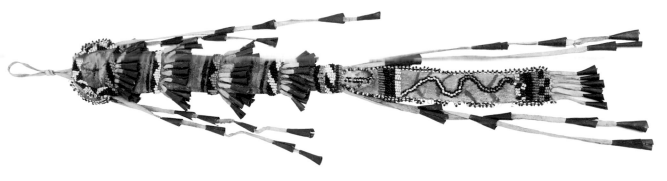

TIMELINE OF EVENTS

General outline of events in Chiricahua and Western Apache history leading up to Arizona and New Mexico statehood.

PRE-1540 — Trading, raiding and warfare with neighboring tribes.

1540–1821 — Trading, raiding and warfare with Spanish; on-going relationships with neighboring tribes.

1821–1846 — Trading, raiding and warfare with Mexicans; on-going relationships with neighboring tribes.

1848–1861 — Trading, raiding and warfare with Americans; forced cultural change; on-going relationships with neighboring tribes.

1861 — **BASCOM AFFAIR**
Cochise wrongly accused of a kidnapping; initiates 25 years of Apache Wars.

1862 — **BATTLE OF APACHE PASS**
Conflict along the Overland Stage route.

1863 — Capture, torture and killing of Mangas Coloradas.

1864–1870 — Establishment of permanent U.S. Military posts in Western Apache lands.

1864 — Camp Verde (near present-day Camp Verde, AZ) and Camp Goodwin (near present-day Guthrie, AZ)

1865 — Camp Grant (near present-day Dudleyville, AZ)

1870 — Camp Apache (present-day Fort Apache)

1870s — Establishment of reservations in Arizona and New Mexico.

1871 — **CAMP GRANT MASSACRE**
Murder of 144 Aravaipa and Pinal Apache women and children by Tucson residents and Tohono O'odham allies on Aravaipa Creek, Central Arizona.

1871 — **WHITE MOUNTAIN APACHE RESERVATION ESTABLISHED**

1871 — First Apache Scouts enlist to engage in Tonto Basin Campaign under General George Crook.

1872–1876 — **CHIRICAHUA APACHE RESERVATION NEAR DRAGOON, AZ**

1875 — **SAN CARLOS RESERVATION ESTABLISHED**

1875–1877	Consolidation of all Apaches and Yavapai on San Carlos Reservation; extinguishment of other Apache reservations.	**1894–1913**	Chiricahua Apache relocated and settled at Fort Sill, Oklahoma.
1881	**BATTLE OF CIBECUE CREEK** Arrest and killing of a medicine man sets off battle; causes great unrest and fear among Apache on the reservation; 700 Chiricahua Apaches flee into Mexico.	**1909**	**CAMP VERDE RESERVATION ESTABLISHED FOR YAVAPAI & DILZHE'E (TONTO) APACHE**
		1912	**ARIZONA & NEW MEXICO STATEHOOD**
1883	**MESCALERO APACHE RESERVATION ESTABLISHED**	**1913–1914**	Release of Chiricahua Apache prisoners of war to settlements in Oklahoma and on Mescalero Reservation in New Mexico.
1883	General George Crook with 200 Apache Scouts pursue Apache resistors in Mexico; some Chiricahua Apaches return to reservation.		
1885	Chiricahua Apache leave the reservation and retreat into Mexico.	**1922**	Apache Scouts from Fort Apache reassigned to Fort Huachuca.
		1947	**APACHE SCOUTS DISBANDED**
SPRING 1886	General Crook arranges a meeting with renegades in Mexico; some agree to return to San Carlos; a small group of Chiricahua Apache escape.	**1972**	**TONTO (DILZHE'E) APACHE RESERVATION NEAR PAYSON, AZ**
FALL 1886	Final surrender of Chiricahua resistors to General Miles; removal of all Chiricahua Apache from Arizona; end of Apache Wars.	**1986**	Centennial of cessation of hostilities between Chiricahua Apache and U.S.; revisitation to Arizona by Chiricahua Apache; first official welcome back to the State of Arizona.
1886–1887	Chiricahua Apache imprisoned at Fort Pickens and Fort Marion, Florida.	**2010**	Return of 290 acres to Payson Tonto (Dilzhe'e) Apache.
1887	**JICARILLA APACHE RESERVATION ESTABLISHED**	**2011**	Return of 30 acres near Deming, New Mexico to Fort Sill Apache.
1887–1888	Chiricahua Apache moved to Mount Vernon Barracks, Alabama.	**2012**	**CENTENNIAL OF ARIZONA & NEW MEXICO STATEHOOD**

SECTION 2

INTRODUCTION TO WESTERN APACHE

They called themselves Ndee or Nnee, the people, and then by their band or clan groups, for example, Juniper Tree Stands Alone People. After centuries of relations with the Spanish and Mexicans, the Americans became the "newcomers" in 1848 at the end of the Mexican-American War. Ndee ambassadors traveled to Santa Fe to meet the new authorities. When American soldiers came into the Western Apache homelands, several of the chiefs—Miguel, Pedro and Esh-kel-dah-silah—met with the U.S. officers to offer peaceful access to their land. They agreed to the establishment of a military post on the White River, where Fort Apache now stands, and to a reservation incorporating much of the White Mountain and Cibecue land.

Yukiko Corella, exhibit designer; Craig Smith, photographer
Gallery view of Western Apache section, *Beyond Geronimo: the Apache Experience*, Heard Museum.

The reservations established for the Western Apache starting in 1870 were often badly managed. Bands frequently had to leave the reservation to forage for food or to raid for needed sustenance. Soldiers pursued them and returned them to the reservation.

In 1872, Gen. George Crook campaigned rigorously against the Dilzhe'e (Tonto Apache), utilizing scouts recruited from other Western Apache groups. The government placed survivors on reservations. Beginning in 1875, the federal government began extinguishing most reservations, forcing most Western Apache, Chiricahua and Yavapai, who were not an Apache people, into concentration camps on a single reservation at San Carlos. The stated objective was to more easily control the tribes and to protect American settlements. In reality, it opened up land for American farmers and ranchers. At the same time, the concentration of more than 5,000 people from sometimes hostile tribes on foreign land created an environment of fear and uncertainty for the Western Apache, Chiricahua and Yavapai.

Gen. Crook recruited Indian scouts, primarily Western Apache, to pursue those fleeing the reservation. The Indian agent at San Carlos created an Indian police force to preserve order. Many of the Western Apache remained on their homelands, or returned after a brief period in 1875–76. Tensions escalated between tribes and the enforced regulations on the reservation triggered flight by those resisting, primarily Chiricahua Apache.

WESTERN APACHE IN ARIZONA: THOSE REMAINING

There were approximately 5,000 Western Apache living in Arizona when the Chiricahua Apache surrendered in 1886. Many Western Apache had scouted for the U.S. Army during the Apache Wars. Some also served as Indian police to maintain order on the reservations. Starting in the 1870s, the Indian agent at San Carlos paid them wages for building roads and irrigation systems. Western Apache were encouraged to continue farming, providing corn, beans and hay to the military, and raising stock.

By 1900, degradation of trust lands by federal mismanagement, accompanied by loss of access to off-reservation subsistence activities and elimination of rations, forced Apache families to migrate in search of wage labor just to survive. After 1900, job opportunities opened up on federal projects such as the Theodore Roosevelt Dam. By the beginning of the 20th century, Western Apaches supplied a large labor force for the Southwest.

The Western Apache were spared the removal across the continent that was the fate of the Chiricahua Apache. Nevertheless, they experienced great challenges. After concentration at San Carlos in 1875, most Cibecue and White Mountain people soon returned home, and they and the San Carlos tribe were able to maintain a significant core of their aboriginal homelands as trust lands. The 2.5 million acres that comprise the San Carlos and Fort Apache Indian reservations make up a large part of what is now east-central Arizona. However, the western Dilzhe'e (Tonto Apache) bands, freed from confinement at San Carlos after 1900, returned home to find their lands occupied by American settlers and ranchers. Only through the people's determination were they able to succeed in the return of 642 acres in and around Camp Verde in 1909. Other Dilzhe'e

Edward S. Curtis, photographer
"Apache Nalin," c. 1900
Heard Museum RC 28(1):15

returned to their homelands near Payson and
persisted for decades on land the federal
government had claimed as national forest.
They succeeded in obtaining an 85-acre
reservation in 1972. In 2010, the Payson Tonto
Apache completed a land exchange with the
Forest Service to add 292 acres to their trust
lands adjacent to the town of Payson.

Edward S. Curtis, photographer
"The Storm," c. 1900
Heard Museum RC 28(1).9

WARRIOR'S JOURNEY

At the point that the U.S. military had established a substantial presence in Arizona Territory, some Apaches signed up as Army scouts as a survival mechanism. The power of U.S. forces at Camp Apache in 1870 convinced some White Mountain, Dilzhe'e (Tonto) and Yavapai warriors to enlist.

There were economic and social reasons for becoming an Indian scout in the 1870s. One received pay (about $13 per month), rations, a weapon and ammunition. It also provided a connection with the lifeway from before the reservation, offering the ability to travel by horseback, to prove skills in marksmanship and gain prestige within the community.

Some scouts felt they were fighting to protect their families and homeland. They felt the Apache resistors were battling what was an inevitable outcome—to reside peacefully on the reservation and adjust to the new way of life—or face assured destruction.

Eleven Apache scouts were recipients of the Medal of Honor by 1890. The Medal of Honor was created during the Civil War as the highest military decoration presented by the U.S. government to a member of the armed forces. The recipients must have distinguished themselves at the risk of their own life above and beyond the call of duty in action against an enemy of the United States.

Military service is still a strong tradition in Apache communities today.

Opposite page: **Attributed to D.A. Markey or A. Miller, photographer**
"Alchesay, chief of White Mountain Apache Indians, and his counsel," c. 1870–1895.
Collection of the Arizona Historical Society, 50082

Below: **Markey and Mytton, photographer**
"Alchesay, chief of the White Mountain Apache," c. 1870–1895, Fort Grant
Collection of the Arizona Historical Society, 22752

Full dress scout helmet, 1881
Metal, leather, felt, horsehair; 9 x 16

After almost 20 years of scouting for the U.S.
government, the Indian scouts received recognition
with a uniform of their own. The plume is longer
for the Indian scout helmet and has strands of red
horse hair mixed with white. The eagle plate and
side buttons have crossed arrows to distinguish
Indian scouts from other branches of the Army.

Collection of the Nohwike' Bagowa Museum,
White Mountain Apache Tribe, 2011.x.001

Chiricahua Apache
Doll, 1880s
Cotton, leather, wood, embroidery floss, metal,
wool cloth, wool yarn, horsehair; 5.25 x 8.25 x 2.5

Collection of the National Museum of the American
Indian/Smithsonian Institution, 103285

WESTERN APACHE LEADERS

MIGUEL (Esh-ke-iba)
Cibecue Apache
c. 1830–1874

By the 1860s, Miguel was the most prominent chief of a band of the Cibecue Apache. He and his brother initiated peaceful relationships with American settlers as well as the U.S. military, welcoming them to establish a fort on the White River.

Miguel was known as "One-Eyed Miguel," having lost an eye early in life. In 1872 he accompanied Gen. Oliver O. Howard on a delegation to Washington, D.C. On the way, the delegation stopped in New York and Gen. Howard purchased a glass eye for Miguel. According to Howard's account, Miguel sent a letter to relatives in Cibecue, Arizona, informing them that he would return home with two eyes.

Only two years after the delegation returned to Fort Apache, Miguel was killed in a skirmish between bands of Western Apache. This was a result of concentrating Western Apache groups near Fort Apache, creating tensions which escalated to clashes between the groups.

PEDRO (Hacke-yanil-tli-din)
White Mountain Apache
c. 1835–1885

In the mid 19th century, after feuding with
fellow Cibecue leader Miguel, Pedro moved
his band to the area on the White River that
would later become Fort Apache. Almost 20
years later, chiefs of White Mountain Apache
bands—Pedro, Miguel and Esh-kel-dah-silah—
met with U.S. military officers and agreed
to the establishment of a military post and
reservation. In 1872 this group of non-hostile
leaders was taken to Washington, D.C., to
meet President Ulysses S. Grant. The leaders'
portraits were taken at that time.

Pedro's son, Alchesay, succeeded him as the
leader of the White Mountain Apache in 1882.

Opposite page and above:
Unknown photographer, *Famous Indian Chiefs
I Have Known* by O.O. Howard (1830–1909)
Heard Museum Library and Archives

ALCHESAY
White Mountain Apache
1853–1928

Alchesay, later known as William Alchesay, won the U.S. military's highest decoration for bravery, the Medal of Honor, for his actions during the Indian Wars.

He was chief of the White Mountain Apache Tribe and an Indian scout. In early years of U.S. military presence in Arizona Territory (1872–73), he became an Apache scout under Gen. George Crook to quell Apache resistance. In the 1880s, he went on campaigns following the Chiricahua Apache, who had fled the reservations established by the U.S. government. He received a Medal of Honor for his service. In 1886 Gen. Crook requested Alchesay's assistance to negotiate a surrender from Geronimo's band of resistors.

Alchesay was often called on by the Indian agents at Fort Apache Indian Reservation to help resolve issues between the White Mountain Apache and U.S. government. He frequently presented the needs of his community. His counsel was respected by both Natives and non-Natives.

Alchesay met with three presidents during his lifetime: Grover Cleveland in 1887, Theodore Roosevelt in 1909 and Warren G. Harding in 1921. Alchesay High School in Whiteriver and Alchesay Barracks at Fort Huachuca are named in his honor.

Edward S. Curtis, photographer
"Alchise," c. 1900
Heard Museum RC 28(1):5

NALTA (AKA DAVID LONGSTREET)
White Mountain Apache
c. 1855–c. 1936

Nalta was born near present-day Fort Apache. His accounts of the establishment of Fort Apache (known as Camp Ord) and enlistments in 1880s for the U.S. Army provide rare insights in to Western Apache life as a scout (Keith Basso, editor, *Western Apache Raiding* and *Warfare*, 1971). He joined Gen. Crook on the expedition into the Sierra Madres in pursuit of the Chiricahua Apache.

Right: **A. Frank Randall, photographer**
"Nalta Apache Scout," c. 1884
Heard Museum RC 6:12

Opposite page: **Nalta** (David Longstreet)
White Mountain Apache, c. 1855–c. 1936
Poncho and skirt, c. 1930
Tanned hide, tin, glass beads, pigment, thread;
poncho: 24 x 40 x 2; skirt: 24 x 33 x 2

A special dress is made for a young woman's coming-of-age ceremony. This dress was made by Nalta for his daughter. He used six buckskins to make it. One buckskin was used for the poncho body and two more were used for the fringe. Three more were used for the skirt, one each for the front, back and fringe. Deer-leg skins were sewn to the front and back of the poncho "to show that the garment is truly made from the skin of a black-tailed deer," as the maker told collector Grenville Goodwin.

Collection of the Arizona State Museum, 21329-a,b

SECTION 3

CHIRICAHUA APACHE: LIFE AS PRISONERS OF WAR

The Chiricahua Apache were prisoners of war at military installations for 28 years, first in Florida, then in Alabama and finally in Oklahoma. In 1886, a total of 512 Chiricahua Apache arrived in Florida. Groups of youth ages 12 to 21 were taken from their families and placed at the Carlisle Indian Boarding School in Pennsylvania.

Living conditions for the Chiricahua Apache in Florida and Alabama were deplorable. The forced idleness and confinement, unsanitary conditions and high incidence of disease and malnutrition caught the attention of several Indian rights organizations. After years of

hearings and discussion over where the prisoners of war should be relocated, the federal government decided to establish a reservation at Fort Sill, Oklahoma Territory. On Oct. 2, 1894, a train left Mobile, Alabama, with 346 Chiricahua Apache bound for Oklahoma.

A.J. McDonald, photographer
"Geronimo and Band En Route to Florida After Surrender," 1886
Charles Baehr Gatewood Collection, Arizona Historical Society, 19796

John Nicholas Choate, photographer
"Chiricahua Apache children upon arrival at
Carlisle Indian School from Fort Marion, Florida,"
November 1886
National Museum of the American Indian,
Smithsonian Institution, N36022

John Nicholas Choate, photographer
"Chiricahua Apache children four months after
arrival at Carlisle Indian School from Fort Marion,
Florida," 1887
National Museum of the American Indian,
Smithsonian Institution, P06855

Unknown photographer
"Apache Camp at Fort Sill," c. 1895
Geronimo's Story of His Life (1906), p.87

Although not confined to jail, the prisoners could not leave the Fort Sill compound without permission or they would be hunted down and brought back. At Fort Sill, the Chiricahua prisoners of war resumed farming and ranching. They grew corn, hay and melons on successful farms and sold surplus produce locally. They raised horses, and an initial herd of 1,000 cattle grew to 10,000. The Dutch Reformed Church established a school and a mission.

The federal government had promised Fort Sill as the Chiricahuas' permanent reservation. In 1903, the U.S. military decided to make the post a field artillery training installation. The Chiricahua had to move again.

In 1913, the Chiricahua Apache were released as prisoners of war. They were given the choice of staying in Oklahoma, living on allotments, or relocating to the Mescalero Indian Reservation in New Mexico. Their population had been reduced to 261. Two-thirds of the tribe chose to go to Mescalero. The remaining prisoners were released in 1914 and moved to land allotments near Apache, Oklahoma. These people became known as the Fort Sill Apache Tribe.

Opposite page: **Unknown photographer**
"Apache Indians leaving Fort Sill for Mescalero, New Mexico," 1913
Mrs. Morris Simpson Collection, Research Division of the Oklahoma Historical Society, 4861.2

MAP OF CHIRICAHUA PRISONERS OF WAR RELOCATIONS FROM FLORIDA

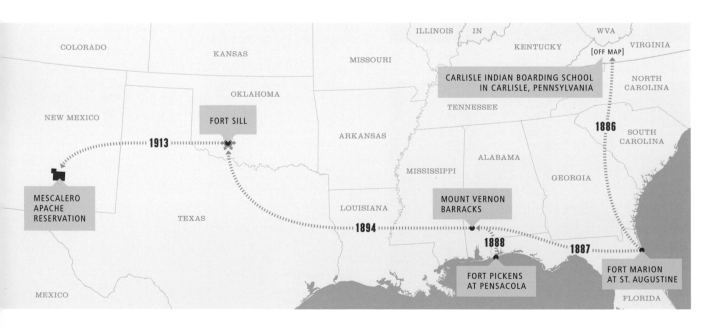

CHIRICAHUA APACHE LEADERS

Unknown photographer
"Geronimo, Chihuahua, Nanne [Nana], Loco, Ozonne [Jolsanny]," c. 1900,
Fort Sill, Oklahoma, in *Geronimo's Story of His Life*, 1906

GERONIMO   CHIHUAHUA   NANNE   LOCO   OZONNE

COCHISE

Chiricahua (Ch'uk'anende) Apache
c. 1805–1874

Cochise was an important leader of the Ch'uk'anende Apache beginning in the 1850s. He fought alongside Mangas Coloradas, leader of the Chihende Apache, in attacks into Mexico. Cochise married the daughter of Mangas Coloradas, Dos-the-she, and they had two sons, Taza and Naiche.

In the late 1850s, as Americans were establishing a stage route through Apache Pass, they found Cochise to be friendly. But this changed when he was wrongfully arrested by Lt. George Bascom, who accused Cochise's people of kidnapping a local rancher's son. This incident, which resulted in both soldiers and Apache relatives of Cochise being killed, launched years of brutal revenge by the Ch'uk'anende under Cochise's leadership.

A temporary peace was negotiated between Cochise and Gen. Oliver Howard with the help of Cochise's friend Thomas Jeffords, a superintendent of the mail line going through Apache Pass. Soon after their negotiation, an Army peace officer parlayed an agreement for a Chiricahua Reservation in their homelands. Cochise died of natural causes in 1874, two years before this land was taken away and the Chiricahua were moved onto the San Carlos Reservation.

GERONIMO

Chiricahua (Bidankaande) Apache
1829–1909

Goyahkla, Geronimo's given name, which means The One Who Yawns, was born and raised at the headwaters of the Gila River, near the present-day border between Arizona and New Mexico. On a trading trip in Mexico in 1850 when most of the men were absent from camp, Goyahkla's mother, wife and three small children were killed by Mexican troops, along with other Chiricahua women and children. Goyahkla would never be the same; he vowed to avenge his family's death. He adopted the name Geronimo in a revenge battle, fighting Mexican soldiers, who pleaded to San Jerónimo to deliver them from the warrior's might.

It was after this life-altering tragic experience that took his family away that Geronimo obtained Power. All things in the universe have Power, and certain humans—medicine men or women—can attain a tiny portion of Power and specific abilities to control forces of nature. Geronimo gained fame among his people as a war leader and a medicine man.

After 1850, the fight extended beyond the conflict with Mexicans to include Americans, as they came into the Apache homelands. In 1876, when the U.S. government tried

to force the Apaches onto the San Carlos Reservation, Geronimo and others led an armed resistance. Newspaper reports, some false or exaggerated, terrified settlers. A series of breakouts and returns to the reservation further agitated other Apaches and settlers.

In 1886, Geronimo, Naiche and their small group of resistors finally surrendered for the last time. The Chiricahua Apaches were put on a train, classified as prisoners of war and removed far from Arizona—a sentence that lasted 28 years.

As a prisoner of war at Fort Sill, Geronimo settled in as a farmer and rancher. He worked as the school disciplinarian, and he taught Sunday school. Occasionally he was asked to perform as a medicine man, obtaining plants from contacts in Arizona. Ironically, Geronimo and many of the Fort Sill Apache scouted for the U.S. Army while prisoners of war.

A. Frank Randall, photographer
"Geronimo, Chief Councilman of the Chiricahua Apaches," c. 1884
Heard Museum RC 6:6

Attributed to Geronimo
Chiricahua (Bidankaande) Apache, 1829–1909
Awl case, 1880
Tanned hide, glass beads, tin, thread; 2.5 x 16 x 1

George Wratten, who was chief of scouts and interpreter for the Chiricahua, obtained this and other personal items from Geronimo. He married Annie White, one of the Chiricahua prisoners of war. They had two children, Amy and Blossom. Blossom later became the mother of Allan Houser.

Collection of Jane and Ed Ulery

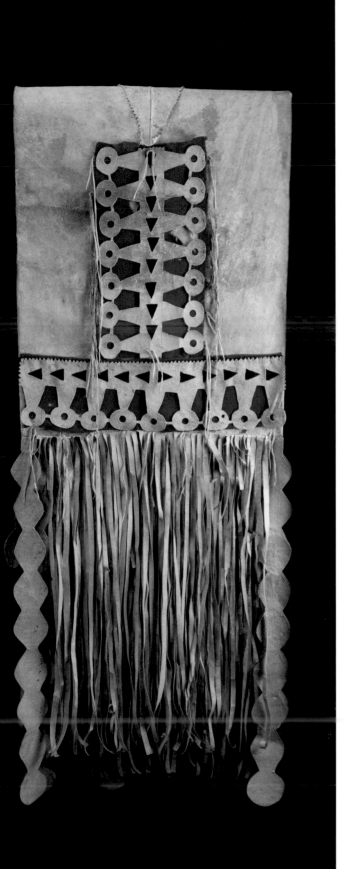

Attributed to Geronimo
Chiricahua (Bidankaande) Apache, 1829–1909
Saddlebag, c. 1900
Tanned hide, wool cloth, thread; 16.5 x 47 x 3

The saddlebag was collected from Geronimo at
Fort Sill. It was probably made for sale.

Collection of William and Jo Elizabeth Ridenour

GERONIMO THE SHOWMAN

Geronimo proved to be an astute businessman and found he could capitalize on the recognition of his name and face. On a train ride in 1898 to the Trans-Mississippi and International Exposition in Omaha, he found crowds gathering at train stops to see the Apaches. They wanted souvenirs, and Geronimo sold the buttons off his shirt, stitching new ones back on between stops.

While a prisoner at Fort Sill, Oklahoma Territory, he participated in international expositions and fairs, such as the Pan-American Exposition in Buffalo, New York (1901), the St. Louis World's Fair (1904), and Fourth of July parades in Lawton and Anadarko, Oklahoma. He sold bows, beaded canes and other items made by him or others, which he autographed for added value.

In 1905 he was invited by President Theodore Roosevelt to ride in his inaugural parade. Geronimo and five mounted American Indians wearing headdresses represented the "wild Indians of the West," in contrast to the uniformed Native students from Carlisle Indian School marching immediately behind the horses. Geronimo stole the show, with the crowd yelling "Hooray for Geronimo!"

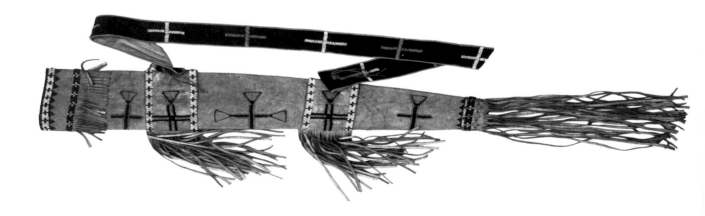

Above: **Attributed to Geronimo**
Chiricahua (Bidankaande) Apache, 1829–1909
Fiddle and bow, c. 1900
Agave stalk, paint, horsehair; bow: 2 x 15.5; fiddle: 6 x 14

Several museum collections have fiddles attributed to Geronimo. It was common for Geronimo to sell various objects, even if he hadn't made them, to bring a higher price. It is doubtful he actually made the musical instruments. Fiddle-making was typically a Western Apache tradition. The fiddles were played mostly in a social context, not for religious or ceremonial use. The painting on the fiddle is very distinct. The four-point star is frequently used by Apaches, but the floral design is unique.

This object was collected by Capt. Allyn K. Capron, Jr., who had been in charge of the Chiricahua Apache prisoners in Florida, Alabama and Fort Sill, Indian Territory.

Collection of the National Museum of Natural History/ Smithsonian Institution, E270085

Opposite page: **Attributed to Geronimo**
Chiricahua (Bidankaande) Apache, 1829–1909
Quiver, c. 1900
Tanned hide, glass beads, cloth, pigment, thread; 21 x 38 x 1.5

While a prisoner, Geronimo made items for sale to army officers and others. This piece shows careful workmanship and perhaps was crafted specifically for Capt. Allyn K. Capron, Jr., whose wife donated the quiver and bow.

Collection of the National Museum of Natural History/ Smithsonian Institution, E270093

NAICHE

Chiricahua (Ch'uk'anende) Apache
1856–1921

A son of Cochise and Dos-the-she (Mangas Coloradas' daughter), Naiche saw his father make peace with the Americans. He also saw treachery, the 1875 closing of the reservation established for the Chiricahua people and a forced removal to San Carlos Reservation. He led the Chiricahuas at the final surrender to Brig. Gen. Nelson Miles at Skeleton Canyon in 1886 and was a respected leader as a prisoner of war. Influenced by the Dutch Reformed Church at Fort Sill, Oklahoma, he accepted Christianity and called himself "Christian Naiche." He worked for the relocation of the Fort Sill Apache to the Mescalero Reservation in New Mexico after the release of the Chiricahuas as prisoners of war in 1913.

Opposite page: **A. Frank Randall, photographer**
"Natches, Nai-chi-ti: Chiricahua Chief, Son of Cochise," c. 1884, Heard Museum RC 6:1.

Below: **Naiche**
Chiricahua (Ch'uk'anende) Apache, 1856–1921
Quiver, 1890
Hide, glass beads, brass, thread, paint; 10 x 31 x 1.5

The quiver was collected by Brig. Gen. Glennen who was in the Medical Corps at Fort Sill in the 1890s.

Collection of the National Museum of Natural History/ Smithsonian Institution, E385915A

Naches " Nal-dhi "

44

A skilled artist, Naiche claimed to have made 20 paintings on deer hide, which he sold or gave as gifts. The subject of this hide painting was the coming-of-age ceremony, a celebration of a young woman's transition to adulthood. The ceremony blesses the young woman with strength and a healthy life. This is a healing time for those attending as well.

For Naiche, the ceremony must have had a special significance. His repetitious painting of the scene with the Gaan dancers was perhaps a way to relive the ceremony and draw on its healing powers. He probably relived the sensory experiences of the smell of the fire and the sounds of the drums, singing, and bells and tinklers on the skirts.

Opposite Page: **Naiche**
Chiricahua (Ch'uk'anende) Apache, 1856–1921
Hide painting, c. 1905
Deer hide, pigment; 25.5 x 33 x .25

Naiche gave this particular painting to the wife and minister of the Dutch Reformed Church at Fort Sill, perhaps as a way of enlightening them as to his traditional beliefs and practices.

Gift of Brig. Gen. (USA, Ret.) and Mrs. Neal R. Christensen

CHATO

Chiricahua (Bidankaande/Ch'uk'anende)
Apache
1854–1934

Chato was a warrior and sub-chief of the Chiricahua who later became a scout with the U.S. military. Until his 30s he fought alongside Victorio, Nana, Juh and Chihuahua. In 1883 Chato surrendered to Gen. George Crook in the Sierra Madre Mountains of Mexico. He became a U.S. Army scout, leading an expedition back into Mexico under Lt. Britton Davis to track down Geronimo.

In 1886 Chato was invited to Washington, D.C., on a peace delegation with 13 others. He was presented a medal by the Secretary of the Interior and given a certificate of good character. The delegation was taken on a tour of Carlisle Indian Boarding School in Pennsylvania. On the return journey to Arizona, the federal government detained the peace delegation and rerouted them to St. Augustine, Florida, where they were imprisoned with the other Chiricahuas at Fort Marion.

Later, while at Fort Sill, Oklahoma, Chato again served as a scout for the Army. He relocated his family to the Mescalero Reservation in 1913, where he died 20 years later in an automobile accident.

Unknown photographer
Helen and Alfred Chato, 1930
Collection of Vincent Kaydahzinne

Above: **Peace medal**, 1886
Metal; 2.5 x 3 x 2.5

In the summer of 1886, Chato led a delegation to Washington, D.C., where he was presented with this silver medal. It is stamped on one side with the head of President Chester A. Arthur. Below President Arthur's portrait the medal is engraved: "From Secretary (of the Interior Lucius Q.C.) Lamar to Chatto."

As reported by Capt. John Bourke, aide to Gen. George Crook:

> "...the incarceration of Chato and the three-fourths of the band who had remained faithful for three years and had rendered such signal service in the pursuit of the renegades, can never meet with the approval of honorable soldiers and gentlemen. ...There is no more disgraceful page in the history of our relations with the American Indians than that which conceals the treachery visited upon the Chiricahuas who remained faithful in their allegiance to our people."
> (Bourke, *On the Border with Crook*, 1892)

Collection of Vincent Kaydahzinne and Family

Above: **A. Frank Randall, photographer**
"Chatto Chiricahua Chief," 1884, Heard Museum RC 6:3

ASA DAKLUGIE

Chiricahua (Ndendaande/Bidankaande) Apache
1872–1955

The son of Juh, a Southern Chiricahua leader, and Ishton, Geronimo's sister, Daklugie was 14 years old when he was exiled as a prisoner of war, along with Naiche, his uncle Geronimo and the other Apache. Shortly after arriving in Florida, groups of Chiricahua youth ages 12 to 22 were sent to the infamous Carlisle Indian School in Pennsylvania. Daklugie was in one of the first Chiricahua groups sent to this boarding school, which was charged with "assimilating" Native American students.

He returned to his family at Fort Sill, Oklahoma, in 1895, where he married and joined the Fort Sill scouts. He was a close confidante and interpreter for his uncle and assisted in the recording of *Geronimo's Story of His Life*, an autobiography narrated by Geronimo, translated by Daklugie and written by S.M. Barrett, an educator in Lawton, Oklahoma. Daklugie accompanied Geronimo to the St. Louis World's Fair and President

Theodore Roosevelt's inauguration to serve as an interpreter. He worked diligently for Chiricahua Apache release of status as prisoners of war and consent to move to the Mescalero Reservation in 1913. There, he served as chair of the tribal council.

Unknown photographer
"Asa Daklugie, Wife and Children," in
Geronimo's Story of His Life, 1906

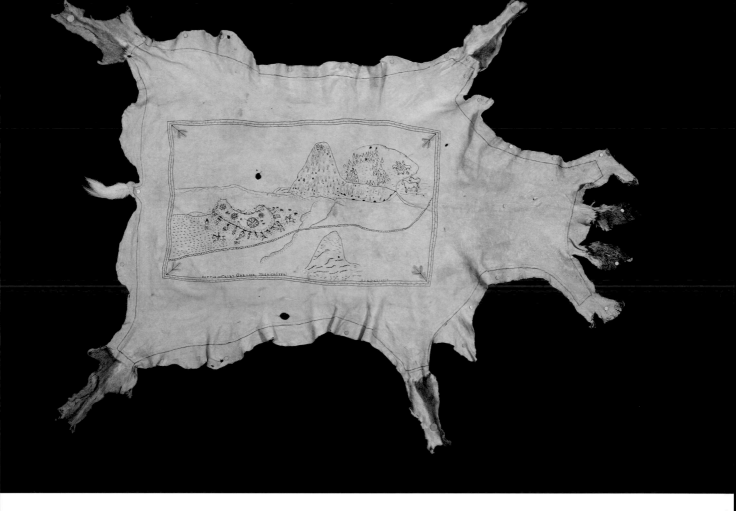

Asa Daklugie
Chiricahua (Ndendaende/Bidankaaend) Apache, 1872–1955
Hide painting, c. 1895
Blacktail deer hide and fur, pigment; 75 x 50 x .5

The hide painting illustrates the 1882 Battle of Casas Grandes, Mexico. Daklugie was only 10 at the time of the event, and whether or not he was present, he certainly heard reports of this major Apache victory, masterminded and led by his father.

The illustration was probably made at Fort Sill when Daklugie was an adult. The painting presents an Apache triumph, when a small group of raiders stole some horses and lured 22 Mexican cavalry down the road where a larger group of Chiricahua waited in ambush. Twenty-one Mexican soldiers were killed, including an important Mexican military leader, Juan Mata Ortiz. Mata Ortiz had been second in command in the battle against Victorio in October 1880, in which Victorio and many other Chiricahua were killed. The painted scene represents a revenge attack conducted by the Chiricahua.

Collection of the National Museum of American Indian/ Smithsonian Institution, 021829

SECTION 4

GERONIMO IN POPULAR CULTURE

Geronimo has become an icon of popular culture, recognizable internationally. Even during his lifetime, Geronimo was sensationalized by the media. There are more photographs of him than of any other American Indian. Local businesses and representatives from Pensacola and St. Augustine, Florida, vied for Geronimo to be imprisoned in their respective communities. They envisioned that Geronimo would bring an economic boost with swarms of tourists. In 1886, The Pensacolian, a local newspaper, stated: "The painted demons would be a better card than a circus or sea serpent."

There have been numerous portrayals of Geronimo in paperback novels, television shows and movies from the early part of the twentieth century to the present. A profusion of commercial products carry Geronimo's name and image, everything from souvenir spoons, packages of chewing gum and cigarettes, toys, t-shirts and postage stamps.

Geronimo's iconic status in popular culture arose most recently when the successful operation that killed Osama bin Laden was given the code name "Geronimo." In that instance, the use of Geronimo's name became a subject of controversy, revealing the emotions and the myths that swirl around Geronimo to this day.

Opposite page: **Postcard**, 1904
Printed paper; 6 x 4

Geronimo reported in his autobiography *Geronimo's Story of His Life* that selling his signature for about 15 cents each at the 1904 Louisiana Purchase Exposition was a profitable activity. A previous owner of the autographed card wrote in old German script, "Signature from Geronimo!"

Collection of William and Jo Elizabeth Ridenour

Below: **Attributed to Geronimo**
Chiricahua (Bidankaande) Apache, 1829–1909
Detail of bow with signature, c. 1900
Wood, pigment, sinew; 145 x 1

While a prisoner of war at Mount Vernon Barracks, Alabama, and Fort Sill, Oklahoma, Geronimo sold bows with his signature.

Collection of the Amerind Foundation

OFFICIAL SOUVENIR
WORLD'S FAIR ST. LOUIS 1904

Palace of Agriculture.

POST CARD

GERONIMO

PLACE STAMP HERE.
ONE CENT STAMP
FOR UNITED STATES,
CANADA
& MEXICO.

TWO CENT STAMP
FOR ALL OTHER
COUNTRIES.

WORLD'S FAIR ST. LOUIS 1904

THIS SIDE FOR THE ADDRESS ONLY.

GERONIMO

Opposite page: **Geronimo**
Chiricahua (Bidankaande) Apache, 1829–1909
Illustration, 1901
Paper, pigment; 2 x 3.5

This drawing of a Mountain Spirit or Gaan was made and signed
by Geronimo at the Pan-American Exposition in Buffalo, New York.
Geronimo took his 11-year-old grandson and others to the fair, where
they stayed for several months, selling autographs and photographs.

Collection of William and Jo Elizabeth Ridenour

Below: **Ticket to Pan-American Exposition** in Buffalo, New York,
1901
Printed paper; 3 x 2

Collection of William and Jo Elizabeth Ridenour

Above: **Goudey Gum Company**
Gum card, 1933–1940
Printed paper; 2.25 x 3

One card of a set of 96 Indian chewing-gum cards.

Autry National Center, 93.74.4.1

GERONIMO IN THE MOVIES

The character of Geronimo in the movies has seesawed from a villain to an all-American freedom-loving hero. The earliest films portrayed Geronimo, and the Apache people in general, as bloodthirsty and lawless. From 1939 to 1950, the films featuring Apache were about winning the West from marauding warriors who must be subdued by American soldiers and settlers. These battles took place in Monument Valley, a location with no connection to the Apache homeland. The Geronimo character in this period of filmmaking was silent and stoic.

The "Apache as villain" filmmaking model changed in the 1950 film *Broken Arrow*. Here we had opposing characters of a "good Indian" (Cochise) and a "bad Indian" (Geronimo). Geronimo still conducted himself as a rampaging savage, but there was an attempt to see the human side of the Apache and a realization of the wrongs they had suffered.

By the 1960s, the film character of Geronimo became more complex, as did the storyline, telling the perspective of American Indians fighting for their land and livelihood.

The 1962 film *Geronimo* changed from the story of American soldiers to a focus on Geronimo as a central character. The casting of Chuck Connors as Geronimo may have been a good box-office decision, but it reflected an insensitive attitude about using a non-Native to portray an American Indian.

The 1993 film *Geronimo: an American Legend* presented Geronimo as an American hero. In this film the Geronimo character was played by an American Indian (Cherokee actor Wes Studi), and the Apache spoke their own language (translated in subtitles). The film was loosely based on a military account of the final negotiations for the Apache surrender. The movie mixed in events from an earlier time and invented a friendship between Geronimo and a cavalry officer. Again, the focus strayed from the namesake of the movie to a story about the American soldiers who pursued Geronimo.

While we wait for an accurate portrayal of the complex and eventful life of Geronimo, we need to keep in mind that Hollywood is good entertainment but not good history.

Yukiko Corella, exhibit designer; Craig Smith, photographer
Gallery view of Geronimo in the Movies section,
Beyond Geronimo: the Apache Experience, Heard Museum.

Posters from the collection of Rennard Strickland

CONTEMPORARY EXPRESSIONS: GOING BEYOND GERONIMO

Through a variety of media, these contemporary Apache artists express their personal artistic creativity based on shared community values and knowledge of the past. Each piece is an exploration of cultural identity. Some artists present a connection to land and the importance of place. They interpret the strength of song and ceremony, and honor family and the warrior tradition. Some of the art challenges common stereotypes and romantic images to find authentic cultural meaning.

Bob Haozous
Chiricahua (Warm Springs) Apache, b. 1943
Older Woman's War Bonnet, n.d.
Leather, steel, pigment; 38 x 86 (on mount) x 22

> "It is a statement of the difficulty challenging people to be Apache in this world today, instead of relying on history or romantic notions to define themselves. Being Apache today is as possible as it was in the past and will be possible in the future."
> — Bob Haozous, 2012

Collection of the artist

Right: In-gallery photograph of artwork.

Allan Houser

Chiricahua (Warm Springs) Apache, 1914–1994
Unconquered
Bronze; edition of 20; 19 x 21 x 12

> "Two men, fast men, quick men rather fight
> and not be afraid at all."
> — Sam Haozous, Fort Sill Apache Tribe

This quote refers to Geronimo's highly effective
strategy of sending warriors two at a time to
engage the enemy, taken from an oral interview
of Sam Haozous. Sam Haozous, a descendant of
Mangas Coloradas and Allan Houser's father, was
a member of the small group of Warm Spring
Chiricahua Apache who surrendered in 1886 to
Gen. Miles. Sam Haozous was a grandnephew of
Geronimo and frequently interpreted for him.

Collection of Chiinde

Photo of Allan Houser by Matthew Wysocki
courtesy of Allan Houser Foundation archives

Oliver Enjady
Mescalero Apache, b. 1952
The Day Mother Shook, 2012
Acrylic on canvas; 30 x 40

The painting shares elements with Naiche's hide paintings, such as the rows of wickiups and people in the foreground. This work is a personal story on several levels as well as a political statement. The Mescalero Apache Reservation is just downwind from the Trinity Site where the first atomic bomb was tested in 1945. The elders believe the bomb has given cancer to the earth and to women from Mescalero, where there is a high incidence of the pathology. Enjady lost his mother to cancer. The artist suggests manifest destiny is still happening.

Collection of the artist

Vincent Kaydahzinne
Mescalero/Chiricahua Apache, b. 1952
Apache Way of Life, 2009
Bronze, edition of 30; 37 x 25 x 7

This piece won best of sculpture classification at the 2010 Santa Fe Indian Market.

Kaydahzinne's grandfather was Chato, the warrior scout. Vincent grew up with Helen Chato, his grandmother, where he heard many stories relating to the history and cultural traditions of his people.

"The piece depicts aspects of the most sacred of Apache ceremonials. The Gaan dance represents blessings for the Apache and all people, as the dance is a prayer for healing, strength and thankfulness to our Creator for everything given us... The entire dance is shown, including the fire, the heavens, star and moon and the singers who sing songs of praise and thankfulness. This ceremony, the songs and dances, have been practiced long before the Europeans came to America. It survived imprisonment of the Apache and attempts to suppress native beliefs, and is practiced today. It gives much strength to my people and is now shared with other people."
— Vincent Kaydahzinne, 2010

Collection of the artist

Dustinn Craig
White Mountain Apache, b. 1975
Diyin and Apache Scout Tribute, 2011
Print on canvas; skateboards: 7 ply maple,
heat-transfer graphic; 53 x 53

"This central piece, Diyin, evolved out of the
need to portray the Apache male as being
visually powerful without succumbing to
the stereotypical Americanized image of the
Apache—a formidable and one-track minded
brute with a weapon.

This Apache man depicted is a White
Mountain Scout. Perhaps during a moment
of calm or a breath between song or
prayer he stands pondering what is most
important—peace and harmony for the
community and a continued existence on the
Apache's sacred homeland.

My depictions of Apache Scouts on the
4wheelwarpony skateboards are a conscious
effort on my part to bring this part of
the traditional Apache man to the young
generation today. So, they might seek out
for themselves the history of their own
community and people and learn to look
within and beyond the history that is fed to
them by dominant culture."
— Dustinn Craig, 2012

Collection of the artist

Dził łigai Si'an Ndee
✦✦✦✦

Dził łigai Si'an Ndee
✦✦✦✦

Delmar Boni
San Carlos Apache, b. 1948
Descending into the Valley, 1985
Acrylic on canvas; 72 x 72

Thematically the painting goes beyond the
Mountain Spirit dancers and their performance at
a particular ceremony. It addresses the relationship
to the landscape. Boni is expressing reverence for
the places in the landscape that have holiness.
These special places are where you take young
people to learn traditional teachings and where
you reconnect with the ancestors.

Collection of Native American Connections

Douglas Miles
San Carlos Apache, b. 1963
Model Citizen, 2009
Mixed media on wood; 40 x 56 x 8

"In the story and telling of Geronimo's legacy, there is tragedy, triumph, struggle, survival, mystery, mythology, romance and reality. Any struggle for true freedom, independence and truth always comes with a price. The reality of who we are as Apache/Indeh people is that we are many different things—like Geronimo—good and bad, positive and negative. There is no other way to describe who we are without living our lives and allowing all of life's myriad influence, thought, heroics, folly and faith enter in and shape us. What are we made of? What makes us strong? What makes us resilient? What have we earned and what will we leave? I don't know but I pray and hope it is really good."
— Douglas Miles, 2/4/2012

Collection of the artist

Allan Houser

Chiricahua Apache, 1914–1994
Ghan Dancer, 1959
Gouache on paper; 19.5 x 29

Gaan (spelled Ghan by Houser) are holy beings often referred to as Mountain Spirits. They are present at curing ceremonies and coming-of-age ceremonies. The theatrical effect of the Gaan dancer performing by firelight is illustrated in this painting, as well as the wonderful movement embellished by the high-stepping feet and flowing streamers with feathers attached.

Allan Houser described applying body paint to a dancer:

> "I helped a bit painting some of the dancers, when I was at home... It was very religious. I like the seriousness with which the medicine men treat the subject, it is a healing subject, and they still have medicine men connected. The have healing ceremonies using the Gaan dance, and it is a very colorful dance."
> — Allan Houser quoted in Seymour, *When Rainbow Touches Down*

Gift in memory of Mary and Pablo Enriquez

Photo of Allan Houser by Matthew Wysocki courtesy of Allan Houser Foundation archives

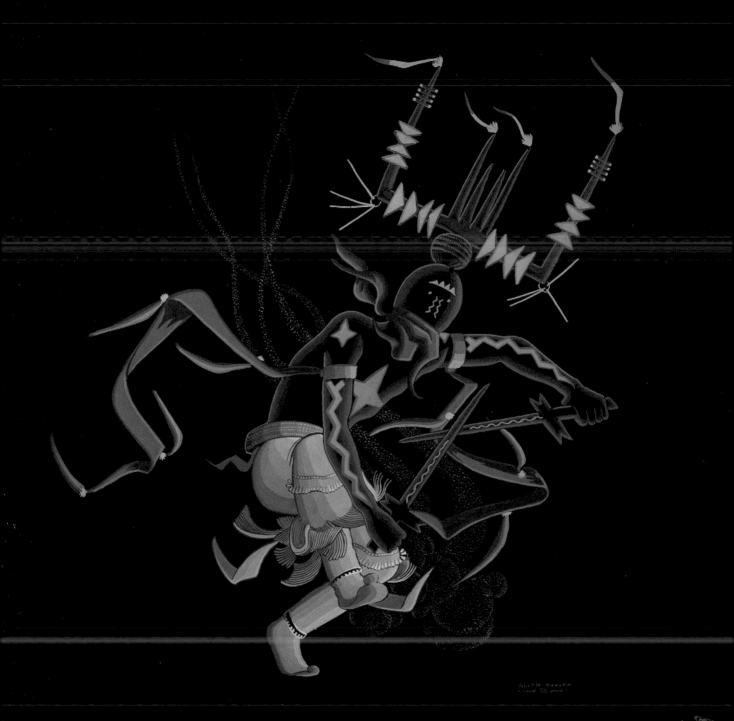

Phillip Mangas Haozous
Chiricahua (Warm Springs) Apache, b. 1941
Apache Love Song, 2005
Bronze; edition of 25; 13 x 14 x 7

"In Apache culture, flute music was an essential
part of courtship, and expression of affection.
The ardor felt by this young warrior for his
maiden is evident as he offers her a love song."
— Phillip M. Haozous

Collection of Phillip M. Haozous/Saayo Povi Fine Art

Phillip Mangas Haozous
Chiricahua (Warm Springs) Apache, b. 1941
Flute, 2007
Ebony, turquoise, feather, coral; 2 x 22 x 1.5

The artist has strong memories of his grandfather, Sam Haozous, making and playing flute. Allan Houser, Sam Haozous' son, played the flute but never made them. He played the ones made and given to him by his son, Phillip Haozous.

Collection of Phillip M. Haozous/Saayo Povi Fine Art

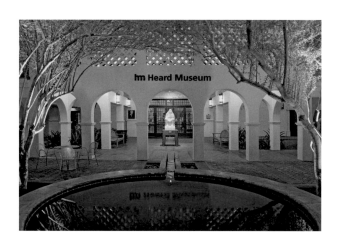

Heard Museum

2301 North Central Avenue
Phoenix, Arizona 85004
602.252.8848
www.heard.org